MOMENTS WITH ONESELF SERIES : 13

FREEDOM IN RELATIONSHIP

SWAMI DAYANANDA SARASWATI

ARSHA VIDYA CENTRE
RESEARCH • PUBLICATION
CHENNAI

Published by :
Arsha Vidya Centre
Research • Publication
32 / 4 ' Sri Nidhi ' Apts III Floor
Sir Desika Road Mylapore
Chennai 600 004 INDIA
Tel   : 044 2499 7023
Telefax: 2499 7131
Email   : avrandpc@gmail.com

© Swami Dayananda Saraswati

All Rights reserved.
No part of this book may be reproduced or transmitted in any form or by any means, electronic or mechanical, including photocopying, recording, or by any information storage and retrieval system, without written permission from the publisher.

ISBN: 978-81-904203-7-2

First Edition : January 2008   Copies : 5000

Design :
Suchi Ebrahim

Printed by :
Sudarsan Graphics
27, Neelakanta Mehta Street
T. Nagar, Chennai 600 017
Email : info@sudarsan.com

Contents

Key to transliteration	v
Introduction	1
What does 'relating' mean?	4
Recognition of facts brings freedom in relationship	15
In a relationship all that counts is understanding	30
A relationship is built only by relating	38
Understanding accommodates everything	45

Key to Transliteration and Pronunciation of Sanskrit Letters

Sanskrit is a highly phonetic language and hence accuracy in articulation of the letters is important. For those unfamiliar with the *Devanāgari* script, the international transliteration is a guide to the proper pronunciation of Sanskrit letters.

अ	a	(b*u*t)	ट	ṭa	(*t*rue)*3
आ	ā	(f*a*ther)	ठ	ṭha	(an*thill*)*3
इ	i	(*i*t)	ड	ḍa	(*d*rum)*3
ई	ī	(b*ea*t)	ढ	ḍha	(go*dh*ead)*3
उ	u	(f*u*ll)	ण	ṇa	(u*n*der)*3
ऊ	ū	(p*oo*l)	त	ta	(pa*th*)*4
ऋ	ṛ	(*r*hythm)	थ	tha	(*th*under)*4
ॠ	ṝ	(ma*rine*)	द	da	(*th*at)*4
ऌ	ḷ	(reve*lry*)	ध	dha	(brea*the*)*4
ए	e	(pl*ay*)	न	na	(*n*ut)*4
ऐ	ai	(*ai*sle)	प	pa	(*p*ut) 5
ओ	o	(g*o*)	फ	pha	(loo*ph*ole)*5
औ	au	(l*au*d)	ब	ba	(*b*in) 5
क	ka	(see*k*) 1	भ	bha	(a*bh*or)*5
ख	kha	(bloc*kh*ead)*1	म	ma	(*m*uch) 5
ग	ga	(*g*et) 1	य	ya	(lo*y*al)
घ	gha	(lo*g h*ut)*1	र	ra	(*r*ed)
ङ	ṅa	(si*ng*) 1	ल	la	(*l*uck)
च	ca	(*ch*unk) 2	व	va	(*v*ase)
छ	cha	(cat*ch h*im)*2	श	śa	(*s*ure)
ज	ja	(*j*ump) 2	ष	ṣa	(*sh*un)
झ	jha	(he*dge*hog)*2	स	sa	(*s*o)
ञ	ña	(bu*n*ch) 2	ह	ha	(*h*um)

.	ṁ	anusvāra	(nasalisation of preceding vowel)
:	ḥ	visarga	(aspiration of preceding vowel)
*			No exact English equivalents for these letters

1. Guttural – Pronounced from throat
2. Palatal – Pronounced from palate
3. Lingual – Pronounced from cerebrum
4. Dental – Pronounced from teeth
5. Labial – Pronounced from lips

The 5th letter of each of the above class – called nasals – are also pronounced nasally.

Introduction

The subject matter of relationship and freedom, although very topical, I would say, is an ancient topic because no human being, now or before, can remain or make one's life without relating to the world. Relating becomes both inevitable and a necessity. When it is inevitable, then one should necessarily know how to relate without being bound.

Two Types of Relationship

I find there are two types of relationship. One is dispensable, replaceable relationship; the other is indispensable, irreplaceable relationship. For instance, you are a son or daughter; the relationship between you and your parents is not replaceable. You cannot replace your mother or your father. The fact of your being born to these parents is already established and therefore, as an individual, you have an indispensable relationship with your parents. Similarly, if one has a brother or sister, it is an indispensable relationship. You cannot alter the fact of your being a sister or brother.

The dispensable relationships, for instance, are neighbours, friends, employer-employee, and even husband and wife—a relationship that seems to be dispensable these days. (Laughter). Suppose, however, a child is born to both of you, then both of you are stuck, please understand. Two people may live a separate life. There may be a separation between husband and wife. Yet, if they are parents to a child, I do not think you can completely dispense with the relationship. Thus, we must distinguish the dispensable from an indispensable relationship.

Besides people, you are related to your own physical body, to your mind, to your senses and it is not a dispensable relationship. As long as you are alive you are indispensably connected to all of them.

One has got to relate to the world

Your relating to the world, the world in general, is indispensable. You can shift yourself from one place to another, but still you will have to relate to the world. You cannot escape from the world. It is going to be there wherever you go. The world may vary. There may be fewer bugs or more bugs or it may be less cold or colder. There may be less sun or more sun. There may be less green or greener. It may be less prosperous or more prosperous, less civilised, more civilised, less cultured, more cultured, fewer animals, more animals, or fewer people, more people. Whatever it may be, you will have to face a world.

You have to relate to the stars, you have to relate to the forces, the natural forces that govern the universe. Beyond these relationships, if there is a God and you have a concept of Him, then you have to relate to Him too. Thus, certain relationships you find are inevitable and certain relationships are evitable, which you can avoid. Now, unless you understand the inevitable as something inevitable, there is no necessity for you to really come to terms with your relationship with them.

What does 'relating' mean?

Let us first deal with the problem of relating itself; we will then go into the details of relationship. One does not have **freedom from** relationship when one is living one's life; one needs to have **freedom in** relationship. One has to relate anyway, since relating is living.

Let us initially accept the view that any relationship is bondage. This is the reason why I have to talk about freedom. If there is no bondage in relationship, there is no necessity for me to talk about freedom in relationship. Then, what is bondage? Anything that I cannot get rid of happily, anything that I cannot get along with happily, is bondage. If I can happily get rid of something, then there is no bondage because I can get rid of it. If I can happily get along with what I am related to, there is no bondage either. If I am placed in a situation where I cannot happily get along with it nor can I happily get rid of it, without a wrench in my heart, without a hurt, definitely that relationship is a binding relationship.

The world is wide and you can always put a distance from someone. You need not say, "Get lost." There are new and decent expressions like, "I think we require space." (Laughter). In fact, when you say you require space the meaning is the same: "get lost." Now this is not easily done even though it is said all right. There is now space between the two individuals. Does it really free the persons totally? In his or her heart, is he or she completely free from the pangs of separation? In any separation, even if it is legalised, there is always something that is left lingering. The person is not the same. The person may be wiser, but at the same time not the same person. In every separation there is something lost, something gained.

LACK OF FREEDOM IN A RELATIONSHIP CREATES DESPAIR

I do not see total freedom in a relationship wherein one is not happy relating totally or one is unhappy getting rid of the object of relationship. This is exactly what is called bondage. Such a situation creates frustration, despair, sorrow and so on. It means that in every relationship there is always a demand on the part of the persons concerned; each one has certain demands. These demands, we can say, are one's own likes and dislikes.

NO ONE IS FREE FROM LIKES AND DISLIKES

In Sanskrit a 'like' is called *rāga*, and a dislike is called '*dveṣa*'. These likes and dislikes form the personality of every person, making him or her unique. Although each one lives and grows with another person, his or her psyche is unique. Twins, for example, are born at the same time to the same parents; grow up under the same roof. Both go to the same school, wear the same dress, eat the same food, the environment is identical; and yet, you will find that one likes football, the other baseball. One likes bananas while the other does not care for them; each one has some peculiar likes and dislikes. So, there is uniqueness, individuality about each person that is determined by one's personal likes and dislikes. Even an enlightened *mahātmā*, has his personal preferences. Then, we have our own concepts of people based on our likes and dislikes. One interprets the world, and even God in terms of one's likes and dislikes.

ONE IS RELATED EVEN BEFORE ONE IS BORN

The question now is, as a person, am I born as a social being? Or was I straightaway created by God immaculately and dropped here from heaven? No, I was not dropped like that from heaven to come here and find that I was all alone. I find that even before I came to know, people are relating to me. I did not know anything about them, yet people began relating to me: "This is my son," one said.

" This is my grandson," the other said. People around were claiming me to be related to them, as brother, as neighbour, as cousin, as nephew—all forms of relationship were already there; I did not know anything about them. I was just lying on my back and looking at the world and everyone comes and... (Swamiji pinches his cheeks - laughter). They are all relating to me in a special way, but I did not know them.

Later, I come to recognise who they are; that this person is my mother, my father, my uncle, my cousin, my nephew and so on. Thus, I am born related; I live related. Even when I die I am told, according to the scriptures, I remain related, perhaps related to something else. Born as we are, relationship is something unavoidable in the relative world.

BORN, ONE CANNOT AVOID 'RELATING'

You can never live a life unrelated, although you can be alive unrelated, when you are asleep, for instance. In sleep you are not related to the world or its situations; you are not related to your mother or father, much less are you related to time and space. In fact you die to all forms of relationship when you are either completely asleep or in a state of coma. However, as soon as you are awake, either to your dream world or to the waking world, you are related. In dream you are related to the dream world, a world that is no better than this world. There again, there are some people whom you choose to be with, some you want to avoid, certain situations you like to have, and certain situations you want to avoid. Again, in dream also you find there are fears, anxieties, cravings, longings, joys, and sorrows. So, whether I am awake to this physical world or to my own memories, I am an individual relating to situations. This is how life is. You are here cast among a lot of people; you are an individual not born alone, but born related.

C̲a̲n̲ o̲n̲e̲ b̲e̲ f̲r̲e̲e̲ i̲n̲ r̲e̲l̲a̲t̲i̲n̲g̲?

There is inevitability of various forms of relationships in this life. If there is inevitability of relating, then the question is, "Can I be free in relating?"

I do not think we can be free in relationships as long as one's likes and dislikes come into play. This is because I am my likes and dislikes. When I relate to people with my likes and dislikes, it means that the likes and dislikes are I.

One can never give up one's preferences at will and then relate to another. If I give up my likes and dislikes, perhaps, nobody will like me.

In fact, people like me because they think that I have some likes and dislikes which agree with their own likes and dislikes. Nobody likes a person who has no likes or dislikes, who is like a stone. If, for instance, a man is in coma, he definitely cannot have likes and dislikes; but who will declare love for such a person? Can anyone say, "I love you because you are in a state of coma. You do not harm me; you do not curse me. I do not have any problem in dealing with you. If I call you names you do not react, therefore I love you?" Although, in America to have a stone as a pet was popular at one time, a pet rock. How can you pet a rock? (Laughter) "Come on, now it is time for you to sleep, come on sleep. Come on, it is time for you to wake up, please wake up." Then, they invented a pet rock mate (laughter) because they thought it is not possible for the pet rock to remain without a partner! (Laughter).

INTERRELATING TO A PERSON IS RELATIONSHIP

When I relate to a person, definitely, he or she cannot be an inert object. The person whom I relate to is not merely a comatose-breathing-conscious being but a person who breathes life, a person who has certain likes and dislikes and who is the personality, who has individuality; it is this person that people interrelate.

These are the persons who interrelate and this interrelation is what we call relationship.

LIKES AND DISLIKES BECOME THE SCALES OF JUDGEMENT IN RELATING

Further, when I relate to someone, I am definitely going to bring into that relationship, my likes and dislikes. It is an inevitable factor. Please understand, relating is inevitable and that while I relate I am going to bring out my individuality, which is the individual who has his or her personal likes and dislikes at the time of relating. Of course, these likes and dislikes keep changing time-to-time, but at any given time they are there. So, when I relate to a person I am going to look at him or her through the scales of my likes and dislikes. While I am aware of some of these likes and dislikes, others are not even known to me clearly. That is why I like a person without any reason, and sometimes I dislike a person without any reason. This is called motiveless malignity, which means I can be negative towards a person without motive. Thus, I am attracted to someone while I do not seem to care for another. It means that there are distinct likes and dislikes, which I may not even know what they are. This is why I seem to be attracted to one person, and if that person asks me, "Why do you like me?"

I do not have an answer. When he or she persistently questions me, I begin to invent stories, since I do not know the exact reason why I like that person.

It is, therefore, very clear that I bring to bear upon my relationships, my likes and dislikes, and the person I relate to can either fulfil or not fulfil these likes and dislikes. More often than not, they do not. In fact, nobody can completely meet another's likes and dislikes. It is impossible. Not even God can fulfil one's all likes and dislikes, since they keep changing. It looks to me therefore these relationships are doomed to be binding, since they cannot meet my likes and dislikes. Thus, I find every relationship falling short in some way or the other; there is unavoidable tension in each of them. The relationship is indeed binding.

When certain likes and dislikes are met with, you like the person, you then love the person. But there are certain other things that are not met with, what does one do? Now, if you do not like he person totally, there is no problem. You can always say the world is wide enough to accommodate both of us in our own spaces. If you totally like the person there is no problem either, because you like everything about the person. You like his form, his nose, his eyes, his height, his shoulders, you like his way of dress;

he puts on a shirt which he does not button and you like that, including the chain; in fact you like macho. This is what you think! You think you like him totally until you marry the person, (laughter) until you live with him.

There is no such thing as liking a person totally. "His looks I like; his emotions are so real and deep— I love them. His thinking is brilliant. He is always pleasant, never given to moods. Totally I like him." No problem, you can relate to such a person for eternity. In fact, only separation will cause sorrow. The problem arises only, "I like this person very much, but..." There is always a 'but'. It means that some likes and dislikes are met with, while some are not. Where is freedom in this relationship?

This is the reason why some people say that you need to be in *samādhi* to be free. Now, we get a new philosophy altogether, the philosophy of *samādhi*. It means, by certain techniques and disciplines, you can get into a state wherein there is no knower-known division. The question now is, how long can you remain in that state? If you say that it is for half an hour, what will you do when you return? Again, you will have to relate to the world and face the same problems. Therefore, I would say *samādhi* is more an escape, not a solution. You still have to account for the world to which you are related. Then how are you going to relate? Do you think all your likes and dislikes will simply disappear? They will not. If they disappear by non-relating, then when you wake up after deep sleep, a state where there are no likes or dislikes, you should be the Buddha, enlightened! However, nobody wakes up from sleep enlightened; in fact, they are slightly duller. It takes another half an hour to really come alive. (Laughter). Thus one can understand clearly that unless one handles one's likes and dislikes properly, there is neither freedom in relationship nor is there a way of escaping from relationships in the world.

I CANNOT GET RID OF LIKES AND DISLIKES

Now, the question is, how am I to handle my likes and dislikes? They are not like my shirt that I can remove one shirt and put on another to suit the fashion of the day. I cannot pick and remove my likes and dislikes. I cannot beat them out of me; they form me— my personality, my individuality, with all my fears and anxieties. This is who I am; I cannot remove any one of them. The only way is to fulfil them, for which people have to change. The problem is, if people are inert I can shape them to my likes. If my father is made of wax, I can shape him exactly as I want. It is the same with my mother or my spouse. The problem, however, is that they also have their own likes and dislikes that are dear to them. Therefore, how am I going to fulfil my likes and dislikes without changing people? In fact, the very same people tell me, "You better change your likes and dislikes. This is how I am and I will be." Neither can they change, nor can they fulfil my likes and dislikes. Even inert things do not behave as I want them to; a car does not behave as I want it to.

There are a lot of things in the world that I want them to be different, but they do not become different by my wish or will or even by my efforts. Moreover, the people, who have their own likes, are not going to fulfil all my needs or all that I want of them. Since escape is not a solution, and if I cannot remove them, how do I deal with these likes and dislikes?

RECOGNITION OF FACTS BRINGS FREEDOM IN RELATIONSHIP

There is no way of dealing with these likes and dislikes, *rāga-dveṣas*, unless you have something more, more than what you understand about your likes and dislikes, more than what you are right now. Some better understanding, better appreciation of the whole seems to be necessary in order to manage your likes and dislikes and thereby be free in relating.

In a relationship, certainly I am going to be conditioned, limited, stifled, and governed by my likes and dislikes. I want the other person to accept me as I think, as I am, as I do. I want my father to accept me as I am. I do not want him unless I seek some advice. When I seek his advice, and he gives an advice, he should not expect me to follow it. I only seek advice; I will follow if it is an acceptable option.

My father also wants to be accepted as he is. The other expects of me what I expect of him or her. Mutual acceptance is a common expectation in a relationship.

In a given relationship I may not be able to fulfil all my likes and dislikes, for I do not have the knowledge for it, I do not have the skill for it. Even in the process of fulfilling, I complicate it although

I think I am settling. Generally, people always get into a discussion about relationship in a relationship. One does not relate—one always talks, talks, and talks about the relationship! It starts when one is fourteen and it continues until one is eighty-five. Afterwards, one does not talk because one can no longer talk! He or she says, "Let us talk, let us come to terms." All the time there is only talking about relationship, which proves that one has not yet related. In between they get married, and continue talking.

The limitations of communication

Nobody relates. Everybody talks about relationship. So, you pick up a particular conversation in order to resolve a problem; in the process you discover new problems. You try to dig into the other person and then he or she is forced to say something that is quickly followed by, "How can you say that?" A conversation that was meant to resolve, creates problems because one does not have the skill to converse. We do not know what we are going to say and how the others are going to react.

Can you avoid talking? No. It is good to talk, but you should be able to have some control over what you say. Many relationships break, not because people do not love each other but because it is impossible to communicate with each other. It is difficult to communicate.

You love someone, care for the person, but at the same time, well, you care for a few other things also. The likes and dislikes are different. However, if the other person knows very well that he or she is loved, there is no problem. There will be some security and one can relax in that love, but it is impossible to communicate that you love him or her. All that you can say is, "I love you." If the person goes on nagging, "Do you love me? Do you love me? Do you love me?" Your reply can only be, "Oh, I think I love you." Your entire attitude changes because it becomes exacting.

Love cannot be verbalised

You cannot open your heart and show your love. If that were possible there would be no problem. We have a picture of Hanumān, opening his heart, with the words 'Rāma' written there. Similarly, if you can just open your heart and show the name written there, say, Julie. (Laughter). I hope there is no Julie here! (Laughter). It is written all over, in huge letters, 'Joooooolie.' It is obvious that total communication is just impossible. The other person has his or her own insecurities. I will talk about more of these in detail. I am concerned right now with our inadequate skills and inadequate powers.

Inadequate power implies no power over one's words

Inadequate power implies that you have no power, no mastery, even over your own words. You say things that you regret later, "I am sorry I did not mean it." The first time you say that you did not mean it, it is acceptable. But then, you keep doing the same thing again and again; your 'sorry' has no meaning. Then, how can the other person relate to you when your words do not mean much? If you keep on using meaningless words then all that can happen is only separation. There cannot be any relationship. Nobody can relate to a 'meaningless' person.

Everybody is born a free person, but your freedom is my limitation. When we communicate, if you refuse to understand me, definitely, it implies my limitation in communicating. I try my best. I can open my heart and speak; but then if you refuse to understand me, I would say that there is a limitation in my communication. I will not blame you at all. I can only say that you are a free person.

You have the freedom to refuse. I am not able to break through the barrier and reach you; it is my limitation. It is the limitation of all great people also. They could not change people. People remain as they are. Why? Because one's capacity to communicate is limited by one's limitation in terms of skills and so on, as well as by one's freedom, one's likes and dislikes.

The more one understands these things, the more sensitive one becomes. One cannot be sensitive to another person unless one understands oneself well— one's limitations, skills, inadequacies and so on. Otherwise, one can never relate to another person sensitively, sensibly. One will become a go-getter, aggressive, trampling on people's toes, expecting everybody to behave according to one's will, one's norms and values. One expects that the whole world should behave according to one's wishes. Thus, one becomes a pusher in a relationship. Like a steamroller, one goes about destroying people's hearts and feelings. This is not because the person is bad. Nobody is bad. It is lack of understanding of oneself. In fact, the more proud a person, the more ignorant he or she is. Strangely enough, the more humble a person is, the more manipulative he or she is. Remember that well. I do not want you to be proud or humble. Just be yourself. Understand yourself.

Understanding one's limitations and skills

You have to understand your limitations very clearly and you have to understand your freedom too; that is another topic altogether. First, if you understand your limitations very clearly then you will find there is certain appreciation of the other person. Only when you know your limitations, can you understand the others' limitations. In a relationship all that is required is understanding and that understanding is impossible without understanding yourself. It takes understanding of yourself to understand another.

If one talks of mind and matter, one must understand one's mind and the matters in one's life. One needs to look into one's mind and see all the corners in the mind. One cannot allow any dark place in the mind to be there. It has to be lit. There should be no cobwebs hanging anywhere. Unless one analyses and sees clearly one's mind, the ways of thinking, one can never help anybody else, nor can one understand anybody else.

Thus, it is very important that you understand your limitations and skills clearly; that you cannot fulfil all your likes and dislikes. Only then can you be optimistic that you have been successful in your life.

You appreciate the fact that in spite of all your limitations you are successful.

RIGHT ATTITUDE MAKES ONE A SENSITIVE AND SENSIBLE PERSON

There is some optimism there, an optimism that does not allow itself to get hurt. You are ready for it because that optimism is born of grace, a happening over which you have no control whatsoever. At the same time, there seems to be something going for you. Since it has been continuing in your life, it should happen forever. If it does not happen, then that is also expected, anyway. It is but expected. You will find that attitude makes you a very sensitive person, a very sensible person. You can understand others because you know your limitations; therefore you are ready to accept others' limitations.

Understand this well. Unless you accept your limitations you cannot accept others' limitations. If you accept the limitations and you cannot fulfil the likes and dislikes, it will not matter. It does not matter. That is why a saint can be approached by an offender, the gravest offender, any number of times, the saint will be a saint, he will be kind to the person. A saint will not condemn anyone, if there is a saint worth the name.

There is no good saint or bad saint. One who is good is a saint. Why do you call him a saint and then call him a good saint? I do not understand that. We have neither control nor understanding of our words nor of our ways of thinking, and yet we want to relate to another person, to understand the person and want the relationship to continue. How can we do that? How can there be any kind of love? How can there be appreciation of each other? There cannot be unless you see your limitations very well, your inadequacies very well. When your mind and everything about it is very clear to you and you understand that the other person has his or her own limitations, then you find there is a dialogue, there is appreciation, and there is love, which is natural. This is how one has to cope with likes and dislikes in a relationship.

There is no other way of coping with your likes and dislikes because nobody on this earth is going to fulfil all the likes and dislikes; not even God.

Suppose you ask God, "God send me a man whom I can marry, age, twenty-five."

God says, "Okay, noted down."

"He must be five feet ten inches."

" Okay." (This is because she is only five feet eight inches).

"He should be of this weight."

"Okay."

"He should be of this colour."

"Okay."

"Please make sure of the shade of colour."

"Okay."

"It should not be too white, it should not be too pale, understand?"

God said, "I understand do not worry. (Laughter). Okay."

"Then he should have this type of hair, okay? Not too curly hair and all that, I do not like this Afro cut at all."

"Okay, okay, okay."

"His eyes must be of this colour, remember his eye colour, okay? It should not be round like owls. I do not like that."

"Okay, whatever you want."

"Nose must look to you. Look up to you, not look down, okay? It should be up."

"Okay. Everything is all set."

"And then his shoulders must be like this; his hands must be like this and his fingers must be like this."

"All accepted, but what kind of lines you want on his palms?" (Laughter) God asked the question.

"Okay put some pattern."

"Okay."

God made a person to suit all these specifications and asked, "Shall I send him down?"

"Send him down."

The person came down. The only problem with him was that he never thinks, because she didn't ask about thinking. Once again she has to ask God, "God please send a thinking fellow." So he sent a thinking fellow and told her, "No more requests." She said, "I have none," until the man, the God-sent man, talked. He has a shrill voice with a heavenly accent! She sighed, "My God!" (laughter).

Nobody is going to fulfil all your likes and dislikes. You must understand this very well. If that is very clear, then let us relate. I relate to my students with the clear understanding that they cannot fulfil my likes and dislikes. Only then can I relate to them. I never want them to fulfil my likes and dislikes at anytime. I allow them to be what they are. As I keep teaching, they keep changing; it is their look out. I just teach.

Only when you are able to appreciate your limitations, your incapacities to fulfil all your likes and dislikes, can you understand, with reference to relationship, the other person with his or her likes and dislikes and with their incapacities to fulfil them. Only then will you find there is a relationship that can last forever. Forever. Why should it break? I do not understand that. Why should it ever break? When you are appreciative of your limitations and you are appreciative of others' limitations why should any relationship break? It can never break; it will never break. Understand?

Freedom is accepting others' limitations

Now, the question is how to be free in that relationship? Well, the very acceptance of others' limitations gives me freedom. That very understanding gives me freedom. I do not want a scorpion to be kind. I do not want a cobra to be kind to me. There is no kind cobra. A cobra has its own power, let it be there; you stay away from it. As long as you are away from it, it is very beautiful. When it moves it is very beautiful. In its own space it commands respect and even adoration in India.

Similarly, when I see a person whom I am related to, whose likes and dislikes are too powerful to handle, I can be away and be free. Just as I do not go near the snake or play with it, so too, without any remorse or rancour in my heart, continuing to appreciate their limitations, I can let people be where they are, remain as they are. I may not have anything to do with them; I may not choose to relate to them; that is being pragmatic, it does not affect me. If it affects me, then there is no freedom.

I said earlier that if I cannot get rid of something happily, if I cannot get along with something happily, there is no freedom; there is only bondage. As long as I accept and understand the person, his or her limitations, I can work happily with that person. In that relationship, I am free. Again, if I cannot work with the person, I can be happily free from that person, because I accept the limitations. I accept the virtues as well. I accept my limitations to cope up with others' limitations. I have no rancour since I am well aware of my own limitations. Therefore, I am free.

Non-understanding of one's limitations leads to aggression

If you understand yourself in terms of your abilities and limitations, it is then easy to understand another person because there is compassion. When you are aware of your limitations—of what you cannot accomplish, that what you have accomplished is not something because of your abilities alone, that the world permitted you to accomplish what you have, that there are a number of factors involved in every accomplishment, that it takes something more than your limited knowledge, your limited skill to accomplish anything—only then will you find that you are naturally free from being proud or overtly humble. You are just a simple person who has appreciation of his or her limitations as well as the accomplishments. Such a person will be compassionate enough, sympathetic enough to understand another person.

In sympathy and compassion there is understanding

I think we can never really understand another person unless we are sympathetic, unless really we want to understand. We must not merely have a desire to understand but a sympathetic approach as well. Otherwise I do not think it is ever possible for one to communicate to another person what one feels. It is sympathy that makes us sense the other person's feelings. Generally, we think that sympathy or compassion are always towards the lowly, someone who is unfortunate, thinking ourselves to be very fortunate. No, that is not the sympathy I am talking of; I am talking of sympathy that is born of our understanding of our limitations, of our incapacities to do things and so on. When you look at another person with this appreciation, you do not condemn another person for his or her limitations.

You understand that each person has a body and mind, but you have nothing against the body. Equally you cannot say a person is clean or good merely because he or she has a white body. No intelligent person will judge another on the basis of his or her physical body. It is purely from the standpoint of the mind. If a person's thinking, values and the actions based on those values are wrong, naturally, you may condemn a person. However, it is also clear that a person can change.

Each one has limitations and each one is trying to fulfil his or her likes and dislikes. In the process of fulfilling them, sometimes, one compromises the means. The end become more important.

If one compromises the means, I would say that it is either because of habit or because of a confusion of values or because he or she has not assimilated the values; he or she has not thought through his or her values. At the same time, one understands that just as one is incapable of doing certain things, so is the other person. If one has this particular attitude, then one finds that he or she can have sympathy. He or she is able to listen to the other person, to understand him or her.

In a Relationship all that Counts is Understanding

In any ongoing relationship, all that counts is understanding. If you do not understand, then the other person has to fulfil all your likes and dislikes. Suppose, the other person cannot fulfil your desires, then definitely it takes understanding to be happy in a given relationship. You can understand your father, your mother, only when you have that compassion. Equally, the father can appreciate you only when he has compassion. But you cannot change your father anyway. If he does not have that compassion and in his life he has not discovered it, well, it is his life. You need to be aware of this, since this is an inevitable relationship—your relationship with your father, with your mother.

It takes a lot to bring up a child. It is a lot of investment of time, of anxieties, of heartburns, of expectations, of hopes and so on. The parents imagine and visualise how their child is going to be—the President, Prime Minister or at least a Senator. Later, this same child says, "I have grown up now. I am not a small kid; it's my life. Who are you to dictate to me?" There is lack of sensibility. It is amazing how people can be so insensible.

You are not the author of your life

You really cannot say that it is your life. It is also the other person's life. If it is your life, which means that you are entirely independent of that person, then whatever happens to you should not make the other person unhappy. But then your mother becomes unhappy and your father develops blood pressure. The reason is you; just the sight of you is good enough for the blood pressure to shoot up; not only the sight, even the thinking is so shallow. Naturally, when you say that you have joined a new group, they are concerned. There is nothing wrong with groups. In fact, it is great if there is some thinking involved. The parents, however, are simple, conventional people who have worked hard to earn some money to give you a good education. They had great hopes for you and in the end when you come up and say that you are a 'groupie' can you blame them for their disappointment? On top of it all, to say that it is your life! No, it is not just your life; it is your mother's and your father's life too.

I do not want you to change; but I do want you to think. You can continue your lifestyle, but definitely you cannot say that it is your life or that you are independent of your parents. You can never say that.

It is just not true because they think that you are a part of their life. You better understand that it is true. Therefore, you are not as free as you think. You are related. You become free only when you have an understanding of the other person, understanding of what he or she wants. It is that which gives you your freedom.

Let others know you understand them

I may, perhaps, yield to some things; to an extent I can yield to some of their wishes. Equally, I may not be able to yield to certain other things, but at least they should know that I understand. The fact that they know that I understand gives me freedom. However, it is possible to understand only when I have sympathy, not chips on my shoulders. That compassion as well as respect is born out of the recognition that I am not an individual completely apart from everybody else. If this is understood well, I can relate as a child, as a father, and so on.

The child is not part of the parents

As a parent, I should know that the child is not a part of me. It is not a part of me like my hand or my leg. Whenever I want to raise my hand, I can raise my hand.

I can also bring my hand down. Suppose, I ask my child to chant because the Swami has come, the child is not likely to chant. When I visit people's homes, they say, "Swami, my son has learned to chant. Would you like to listen to him?" I reply, "Yes, sure I would like to hear him." The mother asks her son, "Come on, please chant." The child runs here and there and refuses to obey. Then, no sooner I leave, the child begins chanting. (Laughter). He is the despair of his parents. The reason is that he is an independent person; he is not a part of you. He has a body and a mind of his own. There is consciousness. He is a complete, whole person. He has his own will and that is why when you ask him to chant, he refuses. As a parent, it is important to understand this fact.

You should appreciate that your child is a part of your life. You are endowed with the power of creation, which is manifest in the form of the child. That you can create another person in your own image is an extraordinary power that nature, that is God, has blessed you with. It is a great power. We appreciate a pot, some pottery, when there is an exhibition. We appreciate the various objects, the ancient potsherds and so on. That is good, but what about this child, who is the greatest art, the greatest of creations?

A pot cannot talk, cannot cry or walk; it can only break. Whereas, here is a creation that is capable of doing so many things. Further, it is not something dropped down from heaven; it is your creation. You have the capacity to create this person. It is the recognition of this fact that helps you understand that the child is an independent person despite being a part of your life. This recognition also helps you see the limitations in your upbringing. The limitation arises due to the faculty of choice that human beings are endowed with. It is a human limitation.

Our knowledge being limited we have to choose all the way

We have to make choices with the limited knowledge and skill that we have. In fact, a cow is more fortunate in that it does not need to make choices, judgements. It does not require choosing between electrical engineering and electronics. The cow is free. It knows exactly what it wants. It knows what it should eat. It always eats the right thing. Human beings, however, do not know. Despite all our knowledge, we do not know what is edible for us. We may know what is suitable but what is not suitable we do not know. Sometimes something works, sometimes not. Humanity has experimented with food and has come up with certain things. We can be the beneficiary of the follies and discoveries of the generations that have gone before, all over the world, and we can definitely make use of that knowledge. However, you cannot say that you have the last word.

That is why a cow is privileged—it does not have to choose. When we are not sure, how do the parents know what is right for the child? What is right to give the child? How does anybody know? Both parents and children should understand this very well.

Further, nobody knows exactly what is right and wrong except the universal *dharma* and *adharma*. We just go by certain traditions, certain intuitions. There is no way of knowing exactly, nor is there such a thing as 'this is the right way' and 'that is the wrong way.' We do not know these things except that we do not want to hurt another, we do not want to lie to another, we do not want to steal another person's property. The reason is because we do not want others do this to us. These are the rights and wrongs we know. Besides that, we do not know anything else. Further, even if we know what is right, we do not have the power to say the right thing at the right time. We find we are being led, *anicchannapi*, even though we are not desirous of doing something, we find ourselves doing something. Understand that.

When you understand all these limitations, you become sympathetic and you try to understand the other person. In that understanding alone a relationship stands; otherwise it can be a problem. Nobody can fulfil your likes and dislikes. Neither the society can fulfil your likes and dislikes nor can you fulfil theirs. So, what is left out is pure understanding.

We can accept each other only when we understand our limitations; then relating becomes fun. We can enjoy the virtues. Nothing else will work. For instance, the advice given in magazines such as 'How to keep the relationship going, or how to remarry or how not to commit old mistakes' and so on; what does it mean? Does it mean that we can commit new mistakes? (Laughter). You commit new mistakes because you avoid the old mistakes. How do we know what new we are going to do is going to be correct? Such advice is just pop psychology—it does not help people in a real sense.

What helps is only your understanding of your limitations, your inadequacies and skills. It permits you to be compassionate, to be sympathetic, to be understanding of another person's limitations.

Unless you understand, no relationship can last. You understand and you say, "Yes I understand, do not worry, I understand." There is a natural acceptance. There is also freedom. I do not find any other redemption for this problem of relationship.

A Relationship is Built Only by Relating

Another thing I find is that you generally build a relationship by relating, not by talking alone. In some form you can work together, like cooking, gardening, housekeeping and so on. Help each other, and talk less about relationship.

Understand that no person is totally wrong

Relationship can become a cause for fear, because previously one had already lost many relationships and one does not want to lose one more. In each of the past relationships, there was a break, there was hurt. Further, every time it broke it was because of lack of communication, lack of understanding. Very rarely is it because the other person is absolutely impossible for you. Even then, he or she cannot hurt you if you understand.

One important point to note is that no person is totally wrong. Suppose you say that a particular person is a criminal, I shall ask you whether all of him is criminal? His leg, his toes, his fingers, his hands, nose, eyes—do all these make a criminal? Is it his heart? His blood? None of these make a criminal. If you say that it is the mind that makes a person criminal, when? While the person eats, loves his wife, his children, his friends, certainly the mind is not criminal then. So when is it a criminal? Only when it drives the person to a crime. Therefore, there is no such person called 'criminal' in the world.

LABELLING A PERSON DESTROYS THE RELATIONSHIP

You know, every time you lose a relationship, perhaps, it is because of labelling. You always label a person and then deal with him or her. You call a person an idiot, but can you find a total idiot in the world? Nobody fulfils a word totally and so labelling is wrong.

I see a lot of ignorance in the world and very few people really think about these things. We have labels for all we relate to. We try to bring them under those labels and deal with them. We label ourselves too. When you examine any label, no one can fit into it. In a court of law, the punishment is for the act of crime, the benefit of doubt is given to the person. When we understand that labelling is wrong, we are open to understand persons without prejudice.

LOVE WILL ABIDE ONLY WHEN THERE IS UNDERSTANDING

In a relationship, only one thing lasts, and that is understanding. Initially, what you thought as love was ill founded and, therefore, it did not last. The love that lasts is one based on understanding, which includes certain aspects of a person that you do not like.

There is something you love about the person. One has to acknowledge that. One can never completely understand another person. But you will be open, if you understand yourself, acknowledging your virtues and accomplishments, the many known and unknown factors that are the causes, and being thankful to all of them.

A mature Hindu is grateful to his parents, to the ancestors, to the *ṛṣis*, to the *devatā*s like Vāyu, Agni, Varuṇa and so on. In his daily prayers, he is thankful to the animals that live according to their nature, that contribute to his life. He is thankful to the *oṣadhayaḥ*, the plants and trees, which not only provide food to all animals as well as human beings, but also give life by providing oxygen. Such an attitude makes a person objective. It is not poetic or religious sentiment. I am speaking as an objective person, a pragmatic person. I see that there are hundreds of forces; at the same time, I see my limitations. Equally, despite the limitations, I see my accomplishments. I cannot but recognise this fact. This understanding makes me a simple person, non-calculative, non-manipulative person.

There is nothing such as personal accomplishment

Further, I have no fear because I see both my limitations, as well as my accomplishments. I see things happening and I understand that all that I can do is to keep doing and accept the results gracefully, as a blessing. If I do not achieve what I hoped to, I understand that it is all part of living and learning. If I am able to achieve certain things despite the many limitations, against many forces, then, naturally I also accept failures. I have been successful before and given the many factors beyond my control, my successes are more a blessing. I develop a confidence born out of my appreciation of this fact. My attitude is no longer personal, subjective; it is very objective. It makes me understand that there is nothing such as a personal accomplishment.

You can never say that you are the sole accomplisher, that you are the person solely responsible for any accomplishment. If you take knowledge, how many teachers have worked on you? Your parents are your first teachers. Later you go out to learn in a school, college and so on. How can you omit all of them in your accomplishment? You cannot.

BE COMPASSIONATE TO YOUR OWN BODY

Being objective alone makes you compassionate, not only towards other people, but also towards yourself, your body, your mind. You relate to your body. You cannot say that you are the body just because you handle the body. You are someone who indwells the body, whoever the person is; that is another topic altogether. You look at this body and say, 'This is my body, I am someone who is handling and using this body.' Naturally, you have to be kind to your body.

How can you understand others when you are hard on your body for no fault of its own? You cannot be hard on the body merely because it has a tendency to put on weight. Certain bodies have got this problem. Even if you look at someone eating, you put on one ounce (laughter). It is a problem. Some bodies have no capacity to assimilate certain things. So this physical body has its limitations like everything else has. You are stuck with this body. If you cannot relate even to your own body positively, how then are you going to relate to your husband or wife? How are you going to relate to anybody else in this world? You need to understand this well.

You are only a managing trustee of your body

Although, you refer to your body as 'my body,' it is, in fact, not totally your body. You are merely a trustee of this body. Your parents have a claim over it and so has your wife. In fact, she says that she is the better half; you are the other half (laughter). The State has a claim over this body, and so do your children. Meanwhile, the bugs inside your body lay a claim saying that this body is their inherited house. If so many lay a claim to your physical body, you become only a managing trustee. Once you are a managing trustee, you have to manage it properly. The body is entrusted to you. Suppose, your friend leaves his car in your care for two months because he is leaving for India, will you plan, "Why not we go to Florida and come back?" You will never do it. Do you know what you will do? You will keep that car always clean because it is your friend's car. He has left his car in trust. You become the trustee of that car and, naturally, you will take care of it even better than your own car.

It is no different with your body. It is given in trust to you. Your parents, wife, children and so on, own it. If so many people own this body, you cannot commit suicide because it is not your body. It is going to leave many people unhappy. You are only a managing trustee.

Similarly, you relate to the mind by understanding its limitations, its moods, its vagaries and so on. There is an order governing the mind. You understand its fears and anxieties. You do not condemn it and thereby condemn yourself. Thus, with understanding you relate to your body as well as your mind.

Understanding Accommodates Everything

Relating means understanding. Any relationship involves understanding. Problems arise only when there is lack of understanding. If the other person refuses to understand you, well, there is a reason for that also. You can deal with the person objectively.

That is why I said earlier that there are two types of relationship—dispensable and indispensable. Indispensable relationship is one where you have to be very understanding and compassionate, accepting the other person as he or she is. Dispensable relationship is one where, if you find the going rough, you can always say that the world is wide enough to accommodate both. You can be independent. You can be free. You need not continue dealing with the rough weather. At the same time, there should be understanding. Understanding accommodates everything— people, events, even death. The physical body is meant to die, not to live forever. All our forefathers have passed away. They are not hanging around, you know, like ET. The body is designed to last for a specified time and when that time is over, it drops off. You need to understand this well. If you understand the general, it will help you understand the particular. Once you understand the universal, the particular becomes easier.

The universal fact is that every human being has his or her likes and dislikes and wants to fulfil them. However, no one is endowed with all the required knowledge, skill, talent or the power to do so. If you understand this, then you will find it easy to relate because you appreciate yourself. When you understand yourself, you can be compassionate towards others. If you understand your own body and mind, you can understand others'. It always begins with you. It is understanding that really works in a relationship. When you understand, both of you can respect each other's virtues and be kind to the limitations. This is true relationship. Such a relationship is wonderful because there is freedom in relationship.

Om Tat Sat

BOOKS BY SWAMI DAYANANDA

Living Intelligently & The Need for Cognitive Change
Discovering Love & Successful Living
Muṇḍakopaniṣad Vol - 1
Muṇḍakopaniṣad Vol - 2
Freedom from Helplessness
Living versus Getting On
The Value of Values
Insights
Action and Reaction
Exploring Vedanta
Bhagavad Gītā (Text with roman transliteration and English translation)
The Fundamental Problem
The Problem is You, The Solution is You
The Purpose of Prayer
Vedanta 24x7
Freedom
Crisis Management
Surrender and Freedom
The Need for Personal Reorganisation
Freedom in Relationship
Prayer Guide

Also available at :

ARSHA VIDYA CENTRE
(RESEARCH • PUBLICATION)
32/4 Sir Desika Road
Mylapore Chennai 600 004
Telefax : 044 - 2499 7131
Email : avrandpc@gmail.com

ARSHA VIDYA GURUKULAM
Anaikatti P.O.
Coimbatore 641 108
Ph : 0422 - 2657001
Fax : 0422 - 2657002
Email : arsha1@vsnl.com

ARSHA VIDYA GURUKULAM
P.O.Box 1059.
Pennsylvania
PA 18353, USA.
Ph : 001-570-992-2339
Email : avp@epix.net

ARSHA VIDYA PITHAM
SWAMI DAYANANDA ASHRAM
Purani Jhadi, P.B. No. 30
Rishikesh, Uttaranchal 249 201
Telefax : 0135-2430769
Email : dayas@hotmail.com

AND IN ALL THE LEADING BOOKSTORES, INDIA